Toucans and Other Birds/
Tucanes y otras aves

By Julie Guidone

Reading Consultant: Susan Nations, M.Ed.,
author/literacy coach/consultant in literacy development

WEEKLY READER®
PUBLISHING

Please visit our web site at **www.garethstevens.com**.
For a free catalog describing our list of high-quality books,
call 1-800-542-2595 (USA) or 1-800-387-3178 (Canada).
Our fax: 1-877-542-2596

Library of Congress Cataloging-in-Publication Data

Guidone, Julie.
      (Toucans and other birds. Spanish & English)
      Toucans and other birds / by Julie Guidone / Tucanes y otras aves / por Julie Guidone.
         p. cm. — (Animals that live in the rain forest / Animales de la selva)
      Includes bibliographical references and index.
      ISBN-10: 1-4339-0067-X   ISBN-13: 978-1-4339-0067-9 (lib. bdg.)
      ISBN-10: 1-4339-0117-X   ISBN-13: 978-1-4339-0117-1 (softcover)
      1. Forest birds—Tropics—Juvenile literature. I. Title. II. Title: Tucanes y otras aves.
  QL695.5.G8518   2009
  598.7'2—dc22   2008040229

This edition first published in 2009 by
Weekly Reader® Books
An Imprint of Gareth Stevens Publishing
1 Reader's Digest Road
Pleasantville, NY 10570-7000 USA

Copyright © 2009 by Gareth Stevens, Inc.

Executive Managing Editor: Lisa M. Herrington
Senior Editor: Barbara Bakowski
Creative Director: Lisa Donovan
Designers: Michelle Castro, Alexandria Davis
Photo Researcher: Diane Laska-Swanke
Publisher: Keith Garton
Translation: Tatiana Acosta and Guillermo Gutiérrez

Photo Credits: Cover © Shutterstock; pp. 1, 9, 11 © Staffan Widstrand/naturepl.com; p. 5 © Justine
Evans/naturepl.com; p. 7 © Nick Gordon/naturepl.com; p. 13 © Thomas Marent/Minden Pictures;
p. 15 © Theo Allofs/Visuals Unlimited, Inc.; p. 17 © David Tipling/naturepl.com; p. 19 © Pete Oxford/
Minden Pictures; p. 21 © Edward Parker/Alamy

Printed in the United States of America

1 2 3 4 5 6 7 8 9 10 09 08

Table of Contents

- - - - - - - - - - - - -

Contenido

Boldface words appear in the glossary./
Las palabras en **negrita** aparecen en el glosario.

Tree Houses

Toucans and many other birds live in **rain forests**. Rain forests are warm, wet places with tall trees and other plants.

- - - - - - - - - - - - - - -

Vivir en los árboles

En las **selvas tropicales** viven tucanes y muchas otras aves. Las selvas tropicales son lugares cálidos y húmedos donde crecen altos árboles y otras plantas.

toucan/
tucán

Most rain forest birds make their homes in high treetops. There, they stay safe from enemies on the ground. They also find food, such as fruits and seeds.

- - - - - - - - - - - - - - -

La mayoría de las aves de la selva tropical hacen sus nidos en las elevadas copas de los árboles. Allí están a salvo de los enemigos terrestres. También encuentran comida, como frutas y semillas.

seeds/
semillas

Bright-Colored Birds

Many rain forest birds have bright, beautiful colors. The toucan is known for its large, colorful **bill**, or beak.

- - - - - - - - - - - - - - -

Aves de vivos colores

Muchas de las aves de la selva tropical tienen plumas de vivos colores. El tucán es famoso por su largo y colorido **pico**.

The long bill helps a toucan reach fruits and berries on branches. Toucans also catch and eat insects and frogs.

- - - - - - - - - - - - - -

El tucán usa su largo pico para alcanzar frutas y bayas en las ramas. Los tucanes también atrapan insectos y ranas.

The scarlet macaw (muh-KAW) is a big parrot. It has a bright red head with yellow and blue or green on its strong wings.

- - - - - - - - - - - - - - -

La guacamaya escarlata es un loro de gran tamaño. Tiene plumas de color rojo brillante en la cabeza, y sus fuertes alas pueden ser amarillas y azules o verdes.

scarlet macaw/
guacamaya escarlata

Scarlet macaws live at the top of the tallest trees. They squawk loudly as they fly in pairs or small groups.

- - - - - - - - - - - - - -

Las guacamayas escarlata viven en las copas de los árboles más altos. Lanzan sonoros graznidos mientras vuelan en parejas o en grupos pequeños.

Huge Hunter

The harpy eagle is one of the largest and strongest eagles. It has a double **crest**, or bunch of long feathers, on its head.

- - - - - - - - - - - - - -

Gran cazadora

El águila harpía es una de las águilas más grandes y fuertes. Tiene en la cabeza una doble **cresta** de largas plumas.

Harpy eagles build a big nest of sticks high in a tree. There, the eagles feed their baby, called a **chick**. Harpy eagles hunt animals such as monkeys, snakes, and lizards.

- - - - - - - - - - - - - - -

Las águilas harpía construyen grandes nidos con palos en lo alto de los árboles. Allí alimentan a su cría, llamada **aguilucho**. Las águilas harpía cazan animales como monos, serpientes y lagartos.

adult/
adulto

chick/
aguilucho

Birds in Danger

Toucans, scarlet macaws, and harpy eagles are **endangered**. They lose their homes when rain forest trees are cut down. People are working to protect the rain forests.

- - - - - - - - - - - - - - -

Aves en peligro

Los tucanes, las guacamayas escarlata y las águilas harpía están **en peligro de extinción**. Estas aves se quedan sin hogar cuando los seres humanos talan los árboles de la selva tropical. Algunas personas se esfuerzan por proteger las selvas tropicales.

Glossary/Glosario

bill: the beak of a bird

chick: a baby bird

crest: a bunch of long feathers on the head of a bird

endangered: in danger of dying out completely

rain forests: warm, rainy woodlands with many types of plants and animals

— — — — — — — — — — — — — — — — — —

aguilucho: cría de águila

cresta: grupo de largas plumas en la parte superior de la cabeza de un pájaro

en peligro de extinción: que corre el riesgo de desaparecer

pico: parte delantera de la cabeza de un ave

selva tropical: bosque cálido y húmedo donde viven muchos tipos de animales y plantas

For More Information/Más información

Books/Libros

Explorando la selva tropical con una científica/
Exploring the Rain Forest with a Scientist. I Like Science!
Bilingual (series). Judith Williams (Enslow Publishers, 2008)

On the Banks of the Amazon/En las orillas del Amazonas.
Nancy Kelly Allen (Raven Tree Press, 2004)

Web Sites/Páginas web

Mongabay Kids: Rain Forest Birds/Aves de la selva tropical
kids.mongabay.com/elementary/203.html
Watch a slide show of rain forest birds./
Miren una serie de imágenes de aves de la selva tropical.

Passport to Knowledge: Passport to the Rain Forest/
Pasaporte a la selva tropical
passporttoknowledge.com/rainforest/main.html
Make a virtual visit to the rain forest. Click on "Ecosystem" to
learn more about toucans, scarlet macaws, and harpy eagles./
Visiten virtualmente una selva tropical. Hagan "click" en
"Ecosystem" para conocer más datos sobre los tucanes,
las guacamayas escarlata y las águilas harpía.

Index/Índice

About the Author

Julie Guidone has taught kindergarten and first and second grades in Madison, Connecticut, and Fayetteville, New York. She loves to take her students on field trips to the zoo to learn about all kinds of animals! She lives in Syracuse, New York, with her husband, Chris, and her son, Anthony.

- - - - - - - - - - - - - - - - - -

Información sobre la autora

Julie Guidone ha sido maestra de jardín de infancia, y de primero y segundo grado en Madison, Connecticut, y en Fayetteville, Nueva York. ¡A Julie le encanta ir de excursión al zoológico con sus alumnos para que conozcan todo tipo de animales! Julie vive en Syracuse, Nueva York, con su esposo Chris y su hijo Anthony.